EXPLORING WORLD CULTURES

Denmark

By Lisa Idzikowski

Cavendish
Square

New York

Published in 2022 by Cavendish Square Publishing, LLC
243 5th Avenue, Suite 136, New York, NY 10016

Copyright © 2022 by Cavendish Square Publishing, LLC

First Edition

Website: cavendishsq.com

This publication represents the opinions and views of the author based on his or her personal experience, knowledge, and
research. The information in this book serves as a general guide only. The author and publisher have used their best efforts
in preparing this book and disclaim liability rising directly or indirectly from the use and application of this book.

All websites were available and accurate when this book was sent to press.

Library of Congress Cataloging-in-Publication Data

Names: Idzikowski, Lisa, author.
Title: Denmark / Lisa Idzikowski.
Description: New York : Cavendish Square Publishing, 2022. | Series:
Exploring world cultures | Includes index.
Identifiers: LCCN 2020035253 | ISBN 9781502658845 (library binding) | ISBN
9781502658821 (paperback) | ISBN 9781502658838 (set) | ISBN
9781502658852 (ebook)
Subjects: LCSH: Denmark--Juvenile literature.
Classification: LCC DL109 .I49 2022 | DDC 948.9--dc23
LC record available at https://lccn.loc.gov/2020035253

Editor: Katie Kawa
Copy Editor: Nicole Horning
Designer: Jessica Nevins

The photographs in this book are used by permission and through the courtesy of: Cover Alla Relian/Shutterstock.com;
pp. 4, 7 Roberto Moiola/Sysaworld/Moment/Getty Images; p. 5 Elise Grandjean/Moment Editorial/Getty Images; p. 6
PeterHermesFurian/iStock/Getty Images Plus; pp. 8, 24 Atlantide Phototravel/The Image Bank Unreleased/Getty Images;
p. 9 © Hulton-Deutsch Collection/CORBIS/Corbis via Getty Images; p. 10 John Stillwell - PA Images/PA Images via Getty
Images; p. 11 fotoVoyager/E+/Getty Images; p. 12 Lingxiao Xie/Moment/Getty Images; p. 13 Francis Dean/Corbis via Getty
Images; p. 14 Arterra/Universal Images Group via Getty Images; p. 15 PARETO/E+/Getty Images; p. 16 Hsi Fang Hung/
Moment Editorial/Getty Images; p. 17 Westend61/Getty Images; p. 18 Nomad/E+/Getty Images; p. 19 THIBAULT SAVARY/
AFP via Getty Images; p. 20 Martin Zwick/REDA&CO/Universal Images Group via Getty Images; p. 21 Vsojoy/Moment/
Getty Images; p. 22 CLAUS FISKER/Ritzau Scanpix/AFP via Getty Images; p. 23 Thomas Tolstrup/DigitalVision/Getty
Images; p. 25 Jan A Jensen/500Px Unreleased/Getty Images; p. 26 LARS MOELLER/Ritzau Scanpix/AFP via Getty Images;
p. 27 labsas/iStock Unreleased/Getty Images; p. 28 ClarkandCompany/E+/Getty Images; p. 29 Simon McGill/Moment/
Getty Images.

Some of the images in this book illustrate individuals who are models. The depictions do not imply actual situations
or events.

CPSIA compliance information: Batch #CS22CSQ: For further information contact Cavendish Square Publishing LLC, New
York, New York, at 1-877-980-4450.

Printed in the United States of America

Find us on

Contents

Denmark is one of the Nordic countries of northern Europe. Together with Greenland and the Faroe Islands, it forms the Kingdom of Denmark. This small country has a long history. A well-known part is the time of the Vikings, who were **warriors** who traveled the seas.

Other Nordic countries include Norway, Sweden, Finland, and Iceland. It can get cold in these countries!

Today, Denmark is known as a happy place. People there are some of the happiest in the world for many reasons. It's easy to get a great education and important health-care services. People get aid from the government if they need it. They have a strong connection to each other and to their community.

Danes—people who live in Denmark—enjoy life. They love the outdoors and take

Danes are proud to wave the Danish flag, which is red with a white cross. "Danish" is a word that describes something from Denmark.

care of the environment, or natural world. Danes do their part to keep the water and air clean. Many ride bikes instead of using cars.

The people of Denmark have left their mark on the world. They're proud of the country they call home!

Denmark is a small country found in northern Europe. The country is made up of a peninsula called Jutland and more than 400 islands. A peninsula is a piece of land that reaches into a body of water.

This map of Denmark shows some of its major cities, including its capital, Copenhagen.

Denmark's peninsula lies north of Germany. North Sea waters run along its west coast. Denmark's islands stretch east into the Baltic Sea. Denmark

FACT!

Denmark's total area is 16,639 square miles (43,094 square kilometers). That's more than twice the size of the U.S. state of Maryland!

Scandinavia

Denmark's neighbors include Norway and Sweden. These three countries make up the area of Europe known as Scandinavia. Sometimes Finland is included too.

also controls straits—smaller bodies of water—that connect the North Sea and the Baltic Sea.

Water is everywhere— and not just in the seas and straits. **Bogs**, rivers,

The Faroe Islands, which are part of the Kingdom of Denmark, are home to many fjords.

and lakes can be found in Denmark. This country is also home to fjords, which are watery places where the sea snakes between cliffs and high hills. Denmark's fjords are beautiful!

7

History

During the last Ice Age, which ended about 10,000 years ago, glaciers covered the land that's now Denmark. As these masses of moving ice slowly **retreated**, people then

This is part of a Viking ship that can still be seen in Denmark.

migrated, or moved, north into the warming lands. Hunting and fishing helped them stay alive. In time, people in these lands began farming, raising animals, and making tools from metal.

Then, the age of the Vikings arrived around 793 CE. Many people feared the Vikings because

FACT!

In the 900s, King Harald Bluetooth (also called Harald I) became the first king to unite all of Denmark.

The Kalmar Union

From 1397 to 1532, the kingdoms of Denmark, Norway, and Sweden joined together to form the Kalmar Union. They were ruled by one monarch—a king or queen.

they raided, or attacked, other lands. However, they also traded with other groups and built settlements in what became Denmark.

Shown here are Danish soldiers during World War II, which was fought from 1939 to 1945. Germany **invaded** Denmark during this war, but Denmark was later freed from German control.

Throughout its history, Denmark was often at war with its neighbors, especially Sweden and Germany. Today, though, Denmark has found a period of peace.

Denmark had many rulers throughout its early history. Change came in 1849. Then, King Frederik VII signed an important law called the Constitutional Act.

Shown here is Queen Margrethe II of Denmark.

It made Denmark a constitutional monarchy. This means the country has a king or queen, but their power is limited by the rules set up in the Constitutional Act.

FACT!

Danes celebrate Constitution Day on June 5. That's the day the Constitutional Act of Denmark was signed in 1849 and the day an updated constitution was adopted in 1953.

Denmark is part of a group of European countries called the European Union (EU). This group works together to fix problems and build a united economy, or system of making, buying, and selling goods.

The king or queen of Denmark is the head of state, which means they **represent** the country on the world stage. However, the Constitutional Act of Denmark also calls for a prime minister to run the government.

This is where the Folketing meets in Copenhagen.

The parliament, or lawmaking branch of the government, is called the Folketing. Its members are elected by the people. Denmark also has a Supreme Court that serves as the highest court in the country.

11

Denmark has a very strong economy. More than 75 percent of working people in Denmark have service jobs. This means they have jobs that deal mostly with people,

Tourism is an important part of Denmark's economy. People from all over the world visit this country!

including jobs in teaching, nursing, and **tourism**. A smaller number of Danes work in industrial jobs, or jobs that make goods such as parts for ships. The smallest number work in agriculture, or farming.

FACT!

Denmark uses its own money, which is called the Danish krone.

Danish farms produce foods such as potatoes, dairy products, and pork.

Denmark trades with many other countries. Danes export, or ship, many things

Many EU countries use the euro as their currency, or money, but Denmark still uses the krone (*shown here*).

out to other parts of the world. Meat, fish, and machine parts are a few examples. Denmark trades more with Germany than with any other country.

The Home of LEGO

Denmark is the home of LEGO bricks. It's where they were first made. There are enough LEGO bricks in the world that every person on Earth could have about 80 of them!

The Environment

In the past, Danish forests were cut and cleared for farming. Chemicals polluted the water. Wild animals had fewer and fewer places to live.

Deer can be seen in Denmark's forests.

However, Danes then started to put more effort into helping the environment. Danes are planting trees, and wild animals are returning. Eagles, wolves, and beavers live in Denmark again.

FACT!

Denmark was number 1 out of 180 countries on the 2020 Environmental Performance Index (EPI). The EPI measures how well countries take care of the environment.

A Very Green Island

Since 2007, one of Denmark's islands, Samso, has been completely sustainable. This means the island uses only green energy, such as wind, solar, or biomass energy.

The Danish people believe in green, or clean, **energy**. Many homes are heated by biomass—energy from animals and plants, such as wood. In addition, half of Denmark's electricity comes from wind and solar

Energy from moving wind turns these wind turbines near Copenhagen. They then produce energy people can use to power their homes and businesses.

power. This has helped Danes lessen their need for fossil fuels, such as coal, oil, and gas. Fossil fuels pollute the air, so it's good to use less of them.

By 2020, the population of Denmark was closing in on 6 million. More than 80 percent of the citizens of Denmark are ethnically Danish, which means their family

Many Danes live in busy cities, such as Copenhagen (*shown here*).

tree has Danish roots. Some people still come to Denmark from other countries, looking for a better life. These immigrants often come from Africa and the Middle East.

Life isn't always easy for immigrants in

FACT!

The average Dane lives to be around 81 years old.

A Special Feeling

Most Danes believe in a way of life called *hygge* (HOO-guh). This is a special feeling of being comfortable and cozy. Many people think this is part of what makes Danes so happy!

Danes spend a lot of time enjoying the simple things in life with people they love.

Denmark. Even though the country is considered a happy place to live, some immigrants don't feel welcome there. However, younger Danes often want to welcome new people to their country.

Around nine out of ten people in Denmark live in cities. The cities with the largest populations are generally on the country's coasts.

Lifestyle

Every year, a group called the United Nations (UN) puts out the World Happiness Report. Denmark is always near the top of the list of the

The average Danish family has one or two kids.

happiest countries in the world. In 2020, it came in second place—right behind its neighbor, Finland.

Happiness in Denmark often comes from trust. Danes trust each other and their government to do what's right. They're willing to pay higher taxes because they know that money will be used

FACT!

Taxes in Denmark pay for many services, including day care for young children.

Danes Love to Learn

School is a big part of life for kids in Denmark. Most Danish kids go to kindergarten when they're three years old. Education in Denmark is free through college.

to help people who need it. For example, the Danish government funds, or pays for, a national system of health care. This helps Danes stay healthy and happy.

During the **COVID-19 pandemic**, students in Denmark often had their classes outside to stay safer.

The idea of *hygge* also plays a big part in the Danish lifestyle. Danes love to spend time relaxing with family and friends. This means they rest or do easy things they enjoy with people they love.

Religion

The Christian religion, or belief system, came to Denmark more than 1,000 years ago. Today, it's still the most popular religion in Denmark.

Christian churches can be found all over Denmark.

Most Danes who belong to a church belong to the Evangelical-Lutheran Church of Denmark, which is the official state church. Denmark's monarch is the head of this branch of the Christian religion.

The Constitutional Act of Denmark says that

FACT!

Islam is the most common non-Christian religion practiced in Denmark.

people are free to practice whatever religion they choose—or none at all. Most Danes only go to church on special days, such as Christmas Eve. People also attend church

Grundtvigs Kirke (also known as Grundtvig's Church) is one of the most famous churches in Copenhagen.

to get married or to baptize their children, formally bringing them into the church community. Funerals also take place in churches to honor loved ones who have died.

Women in the Church

Not all churches allow women to be pastors, or leaders. However, the Evangelical-Lutheran Church of Denmark does. In fact, more than half of all pastors in this church are women.

Language

The sounds of Denmark include people speaking in different languages. However, one language often stands out above all others. Denmark has its own language. The

This sign shows that the Danish word for Denmark is Danmark.

Danish language is also called Dansk. It's the official language of Denmark and is spoken by almost all citizens of this country.

Although most Danish citizens speak the Danish language, many of them also speak more

FACT!

Danes can often understand someone speaking Norwegian because it sounds a lot like the Danish language.

Not Just Danish

People from the Faroe Islands speak Faroese, and Greenlanders speak Greenlandic. This is an Inuit language spoken by the indigenous, or native, people of Greenland.

than one other language. English is the second most common language heard in Denmark. Danish children learn English in school from a young age. They can also learn

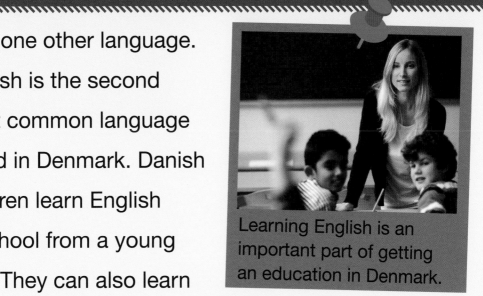

Learning English is an important part of getting an education in Denmark.

other languages, such as German, which is the third most popular language spoken in Denmark. Many Danes speak other languages, too, including Swedish, French, and Spanish.

Like people everywhere, Danes like to celebrate, or honor, special days. There are celebrations during the cold winter months and in the warmer summertime.

Christmas markets pop up throughout Denmark during the holiday season.

Christmas is an important holiday in Denmark, and Christmas Eve is when the celebrating starts. People decorate their homes and make special foods. Families sing and dance around the Christmas tree before opening gifts. They also

FACT!

Danish movies have won awards, or prizes, around the world.

Fastelavn is a Danish holiday celebrated mainly by kids. On this day, kids dress up in costumes and hit a hanging barrel until the candy inside comes out.

sometimes go to church at midnight.

On June 23, Danes celebrate the summer solstice—the longest day of the year. People gather with family and friends and have big bonfires.

In Denmark, June 23 is often called Sankt Hans Aften, or St. John's Eve. It honors John the Baptist—an important person in Christian history.

Storytelling is an important art in Denmark. Every August, the city of Odense celebrates its hometown hero, Hans Christian Andersen. He's famous for his fairy tales.

Danes love all kinds of sports. Most kids in Denmark play some kind of sport, and many adults join sports clubs too. One of the most popular sports

Soccer is also a popular sport in Denmark.

in Denmark is handball. In this sport, players pass a ball to each other as they try to put the ball in the other team's goal.

Biking is a big part of life in Denmark. People bike to work or school in cities such as

FACT!

Kids in Denmark often learn to swim in school.

The Vikings mastered the art of sailing. Today's Danes are also successful sailors. They've won 30 Olympic medals for the sport as of 2020.

Copenhagen. Families or groups of friends sometimes go for bike rides together when the weather is nice.

Bike rides help people stay fit and are good for the environment too!

During the cold winter months, Danes play games or share food and drinks inside. In the summer, many Danes travel to their summer houses. They have parties there with family and friends.

Food

Like most of us, Danes enjoy good food. Much of their food is grown in the fields or fished from the sea. Fish, pork, cabbage, beets, and rye bread are often on the table. In Denmark, smorrebrod is a

Shown here is one example of a popular Danish smorrebrod lunch. The rye bread is covered with fish and onions.

common lunchtime meal. Small slices of rye bread are topped with meat, fish, eggs, or vegetables.

Denmark's national dish is crispy pork served with potatoes and a **sauce** made with a green

At Christmas, Danes enjoy rice pudding for dessert.

plant called parsley. Some people might think the Danish pastry is actually Denmark's national dish, but it's not. In fact, this sweet breakfast treat came to Denmark from

Denmark has many bakeries where people can grab a sweet treat.

Austria. Danish people still eat these pastries, though. They love sweet foods and desserts, including chocolate.

A Danish Dog

Danes have their own kind of hot dogs. Sausages are served on buns with onions, pickles, and different sauces, such as mustard and ketchup.

Glossary

bog	Wet, spongy ground that is often next to a body of water.
COVID-19 pandemic	An event that began in China in 2019 in which a disease that causes breathing problems, a fever, and other health issues spread rapidly around the world and made millions of people sick in a short period of time.
energy	The power to work or to act.
invade	To enter a country to take control by military force.
represent	To act officially or stand for someone or something.
retreat	To move away.
sauce	A usually thick liquid that is poured over or mixed with food.
tourism	The business of drawing in tourists, or people traveling to visit another place.
warrior	A person who fights in battles and is known for their bravery and skill.

Find Out More

Books

Leaf, Christina. *Denmark.* Minnetonka, MN: Bellwether
Media, Inc., 2020.

Markovics, Adam. *Denmark.* Minneapolis, MN:
Bearport Publishing, 2020.

Website

National Geographic Kids: Denmark

kids.nationalgeographic.com/explore/countries/
denmark/

Watch a slide show and learn cool facts about
Denmark from *National Geographic Kids.*

Video

**"Munchies Presents: The Art of
Making Danish Hot Dogs"**

www.youtube.com/watch?v=Yvfv0wmyGro

Watch and learn how to make Danish hot dogs from
a hot dog stand in Copenhagen.

Index

About the Author

Lisa Idzikowski is a biologist and writer from Milwaukee, Wisconsin. She loves science, history, and living near Lake Michigan. When she isn't reading, researching, or writing, Lisa works on her native plant garden to attract birds, bees, and butterflies. She hopes to someday bike all around Denmark and see where the scientist Niels Bohr lived and worked.